WHY WORMS?

Gillian Davies

Illustrated by Robin Kramer

COLLINS

Andrew had a drawing book – a big, fat, enormous drawing book. It had lots of 'please-fill-me-up' pages, so Andrew drew on them with his chunky red crayon.

He drew cars, cats and cowboys. He drew kings, queens and astronauts.
He drew horses, hills and helicopters.

But most of all, he drew worms – lovely, wriggly worms!
"Why worms?" asked his mum.
"Because I like them," said Andrew, "and they're easy."

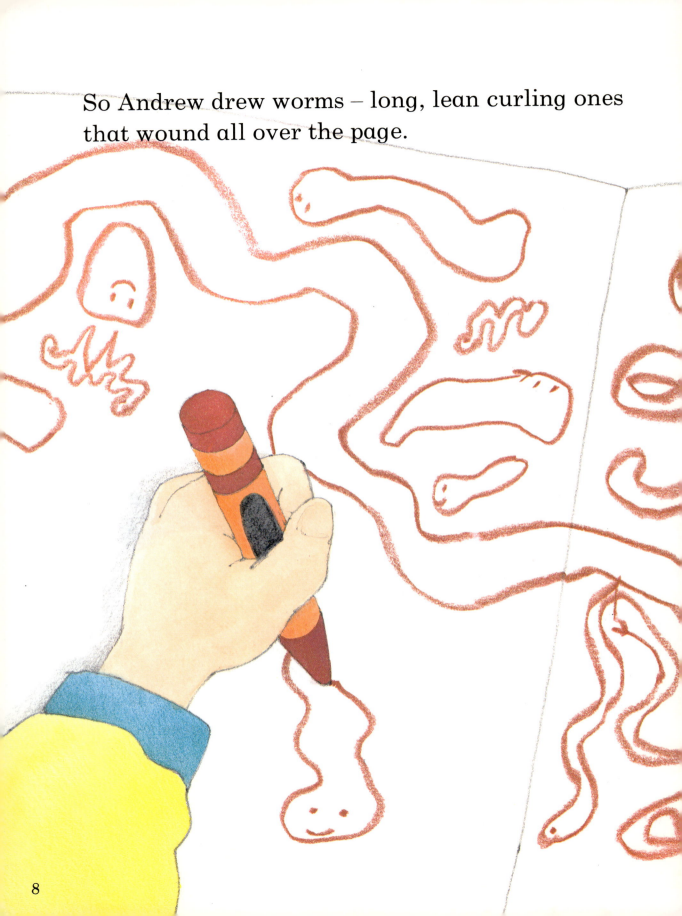

So Andrew drew worms – long, lean curling ones that wound all over the page.

He drew weeny, squidged-up ones, in the corners.
He drew worms on their backs, on their fronts and upside down.

There were worms so thin they tangled up like cotton, and worms so fat they filled a whole page with one wriggle.

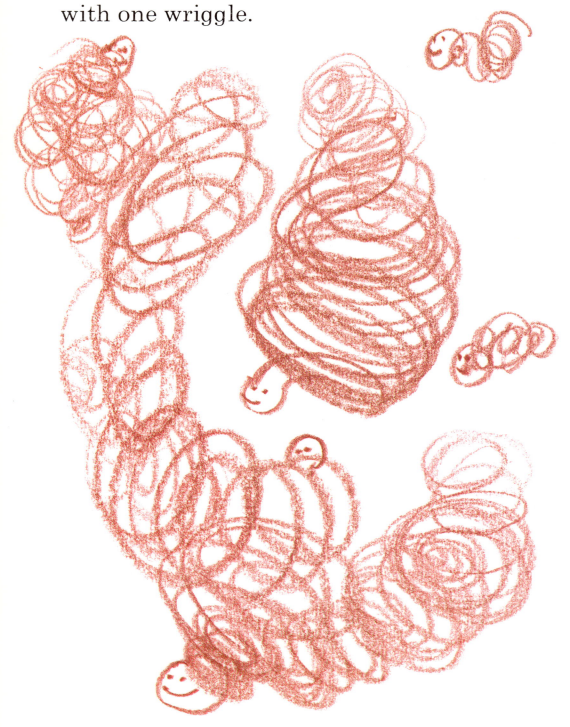

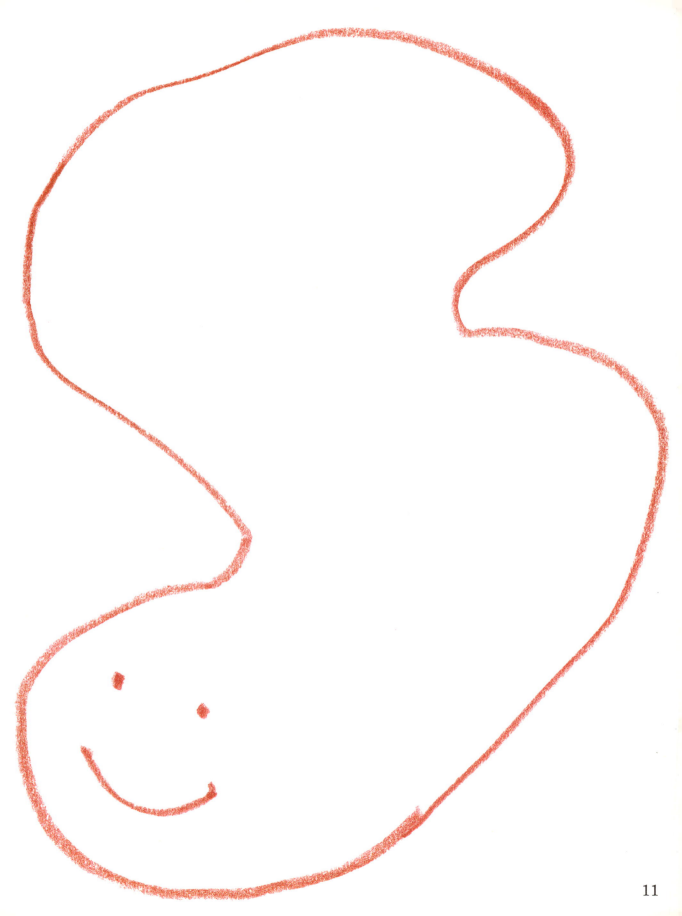

Andrew drew worms in cars, under cats and in cowboy hats!
He drew worms that rode horses, looped over hills and waved out of helicopters.
He drew and drew until there were no worms left and the big, fat, enormous drawing book was full!

Andrew looked around for somewhere else to draw. But there was only the wall – the beautiful, white bedroom wall!

So he drew an especially big, happy worm. It weaved its way along by Andrew's bed and peeped round the corner to beam over his head.

"Come and see my happy worm!" shouted Andrew.

But his mum didn't like the worm at all. In fact, she was very angry.

She made him wash the worm away with a wet cloth.

So Andrew was sad and he drew sad worms on his pillowcases.

His mum didn't like the sad worms either. She took away his crayon – and his pillowcase to wash!

"Time for bed," she said. So Andrew had to dream of worms instead.

The next day Andrew wanted to draw again. "We're going shopping first," said his mum.

And Andrew's mum bought him a new, big, fat enormous drawing book with even more pages and an especially
blue, blue crayon.

But Andrew was fed up with worms now, so he drew . . .

spiders instead!